Animal School
What Class Are You?

by **Michelle Lord**

illustrated by **Michael Garland**

Holiday House / New York

Vertebrates Have Spines

Elephants to pygmy wrasses,
vertebrates are grouped by classes.

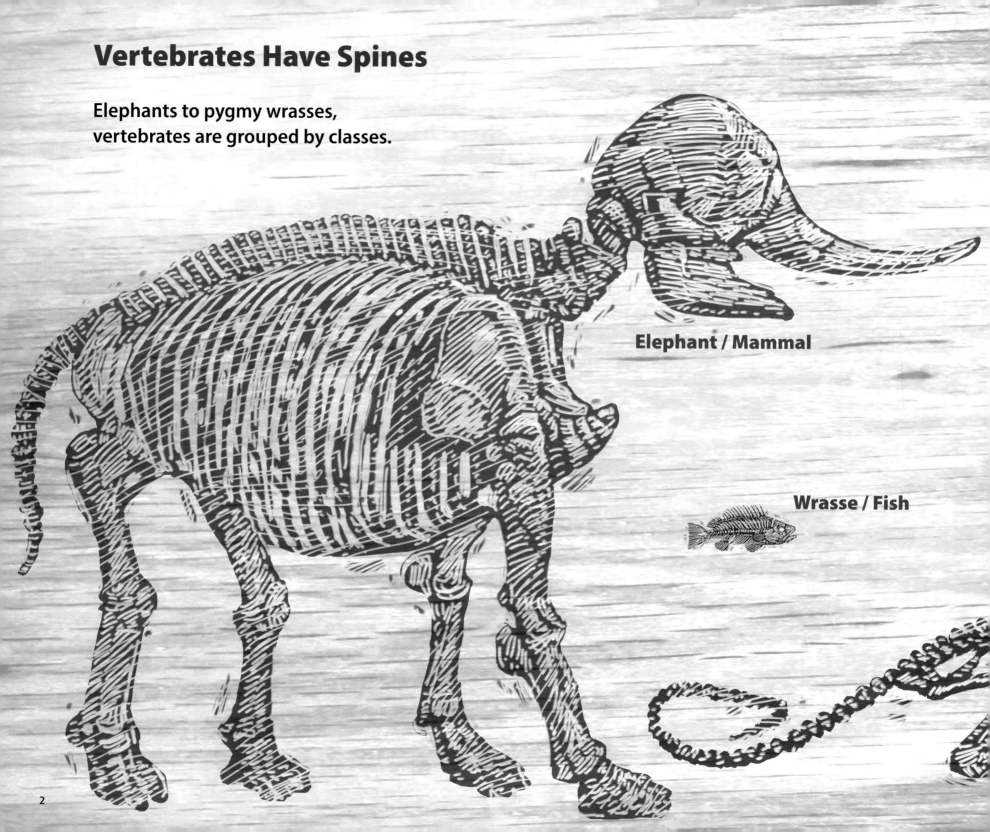

Elephant / Mammal

Wrasse / Fish

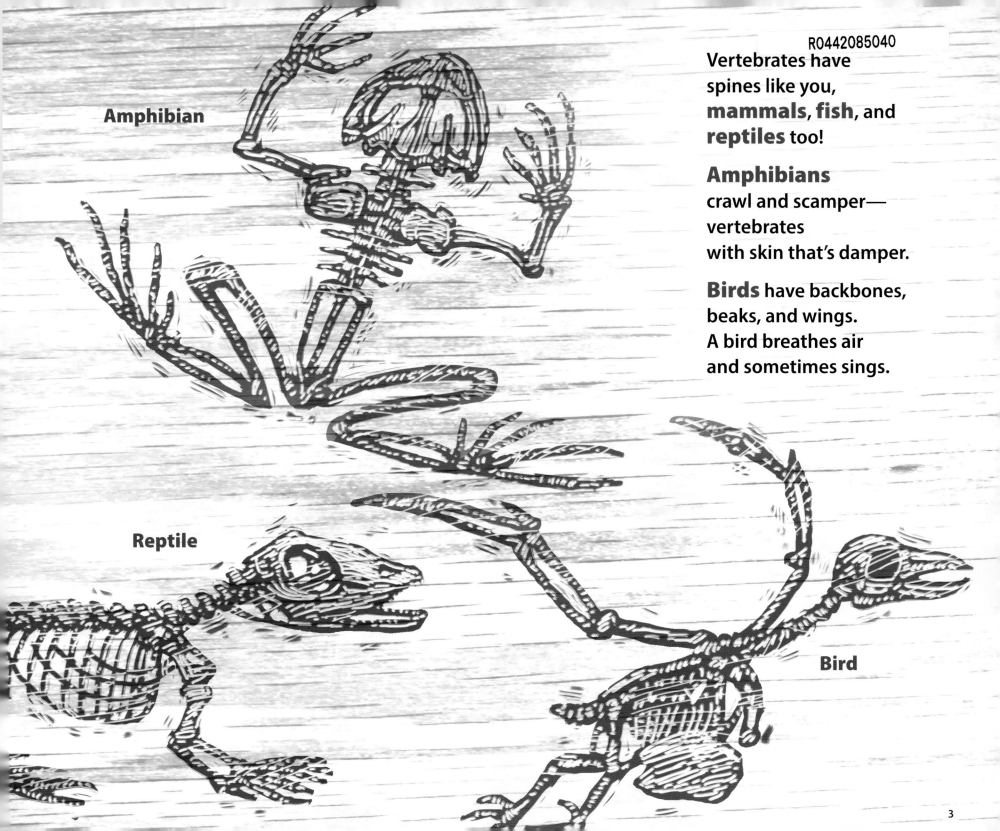

Vertebrates have
spines like you,
mammals, **fish**, and
reptiles too!

Amphibians
crawl and scamper—
vertebrates
with skin that's damper.

Birds have backbones,
beaks, and wings.
A bird breathes air
and sometimes sings.

Amphibian

Reptile

Bird

3

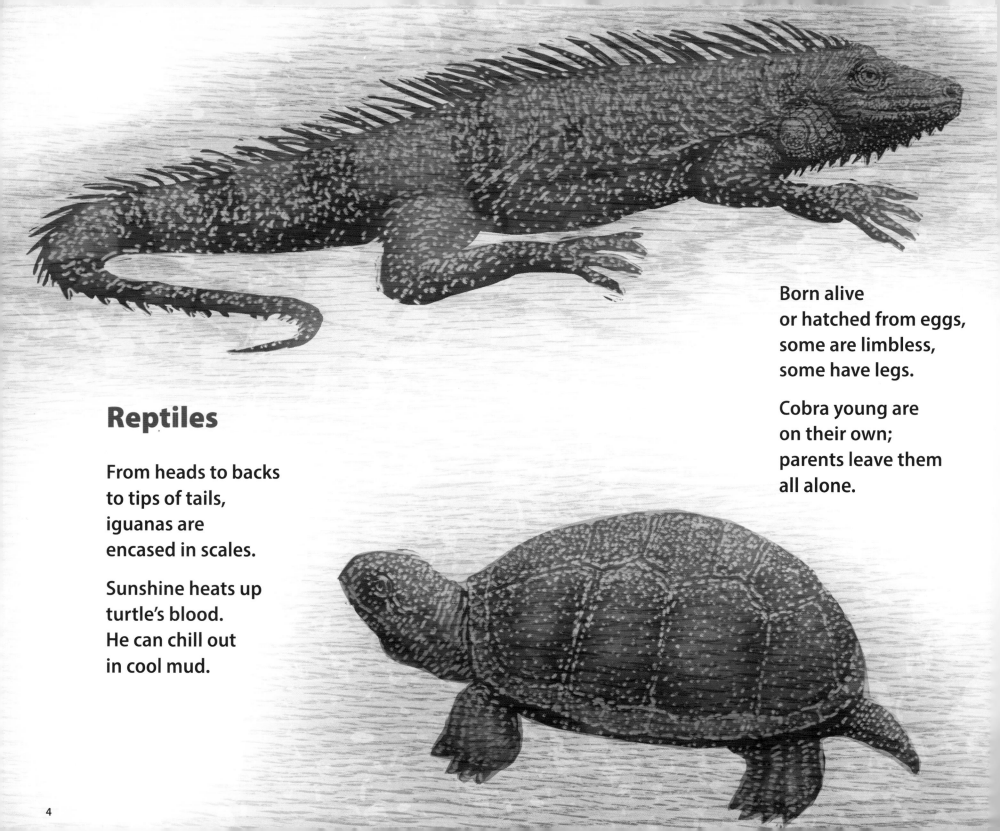

Reptiles

From heads to backs
to tips of tails,
iguanas are
encased in scales.

Sunshine heats up
turtle's blood.
He can chill out
in cool mud.

Born alive
or hatched from eggs,
some are limbless,
some have legs.

Cobra young are
on their own;
parents leave them
all alone.

Reptiles

But alligators
raise their young.
Hatchlings ride on
Mother's tongue.

Every noise
a reptile hears
through covered holes,
not floppy ears.

6

Fish

Underwater,
fishes roam.
Rivers, lakes,
or seas are home.

Oxygen flows
through their gills.
Water passes
through these frills.

Fish are cloaked
in flaky scales,
lacking hair or
furry tails.

Fish

Blood runs cold
through fishy parts.
It's pumped around
by beating hearts.

What helps fishes
stop and go?
Fins propel them—
to and fro!

Fingerlings,
from eggs they hatch—
sometimes hundreds
in a batch.

Daddy sea horse
swims so slow;
in his brood pouch
babies grow.

Mammals

Desert heat to
icy range,
a mammal's temp has
little change.

Mammals

Baby drinking:
milk from Mom
fills his belly,
keeps him calm.

Born alive,
not laid in eggs,
mammals mostly
walk on legs.

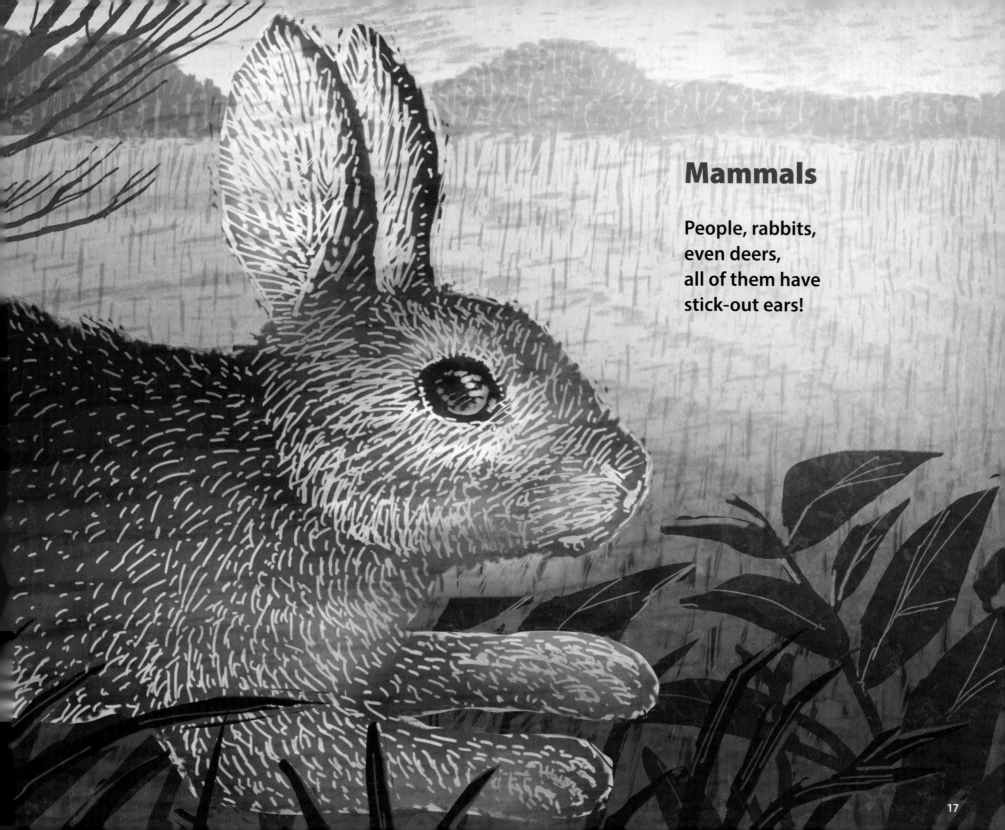

Mammals

People, rabbits,
even deers,
all of them have
stick-out ears!

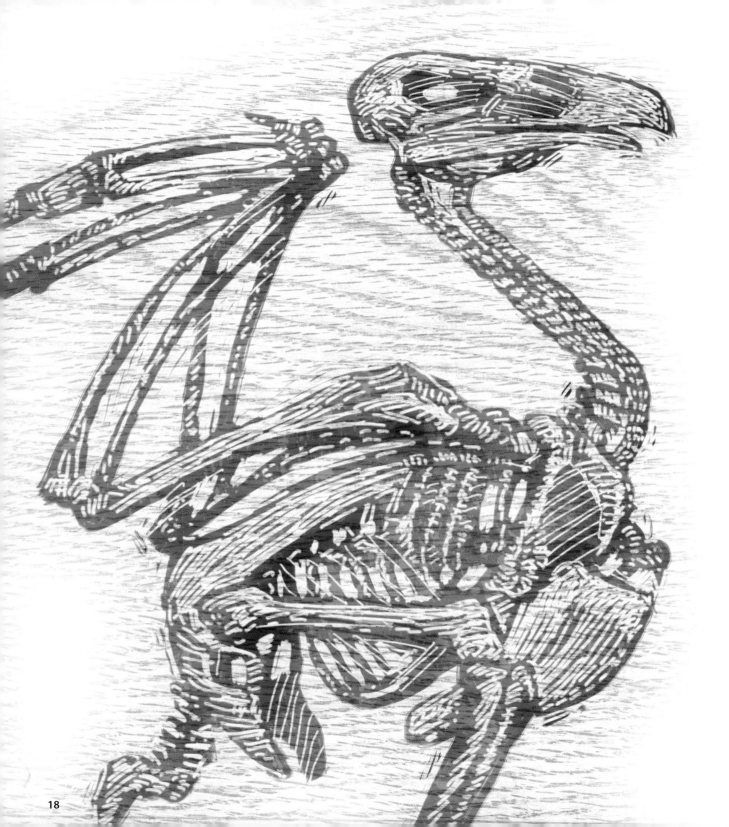

Birds

Hollow bones help
eagles fly.
Feathers take them
through the sky.

Birds

Bright blue plumage
dazzles mate.
Songbird whistles
for his date.

Beaks are used for
pecking bugs,
turning eggs, and
plucking slugs.

Penguin father
sways through sleet
with an egg
upon his feet.

Amphibians

Tadpole gills
will ventilate.
Toads inhale,
and lungs inflate.

Tree frog chorus:
peep, peep, peep.
Through the woodlands
froglets leap.

Salamander's
tail is long.
Skin is moist and
legs are strong.

Amphibians

Newt and toad are
sensitive
to pollution
where they live.

All are born
in water . . . and
grow their legs
to live on land.

24

Vertebrates

Salamander,
cockatoo,
rattlesnake,
and kangaroo,
barracuda,
people too:
vertebrate's
the name for you!

Amphibians	Birds	Fish
Characteristics*	**Characteristics***	**Characteristics***
4 legs with webbed feet or no legs smooth, moist skin neither holes nor stick-out ears live both on land and in water breathe with gills, then lungs cold-blooded many eggs are laid in water	2 legs feathers, wings, and beaks holes for ears live on land breathe with lungs warm-blooded hatch from hard-shelled eggs	no legs scales and fins holes for ears live in water breathe with gills cold-blooded many eggs are laid in water
Some Species	**Some Species**	**Some Species**
bullfrog caecilian newt salamander toad	chicken cockatoo eagle flamingo penguin	angelfish barracuda goldfish sea horse shark
Exception Example	**Exception Example**	**Exception Example**
The axolotl breathes through gills and remains a tadpole, living all its life in water. * There are exceptions in each class.	Penguins have wings but use them to swim instead of fly.	Stingrays do not lay eggs; they give birth to live pups.

Mammals	Reptiles
Characteristics*	**Characteristics***
4 legs (or 2 arms and 2 legs) fur or hair ears that stick out most live on land, some in water breathe with lungs warm-blooded born live, drink mother's milk	4 legs or no legs dry skin and scales holes for ears live both on land and in water breathe with lungs cold-blooded usually hatch from eggs, but sometimes born live
Some Species	**Some Species**
dog human kangaroo platypus whale	alligator cobra iguana rattlesnake turtle
Exception Example	**Exception Example**
Seals and dolphins are mammals with holes, not stick-out ears.	Snakes do not have ear openings, but they can hear.

Afterword

Invertebrates
are spineless things—
lobster, spider,
bugs with wings!

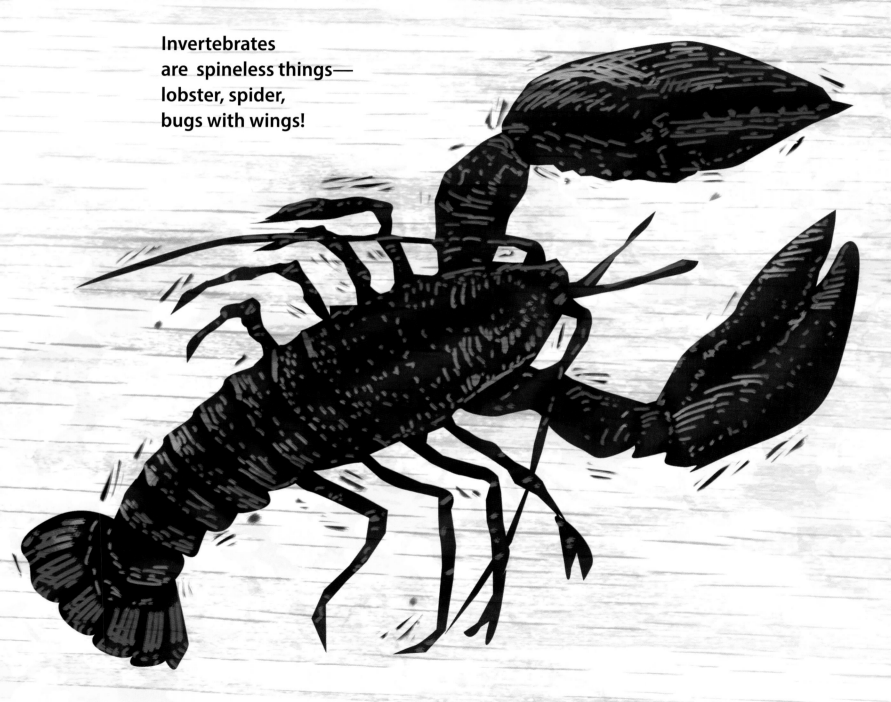

Selected Bibliography

Howell, Catherine Herbert. *Reptiles & Amphibians*. Washington, DC: National Geographic Society, 1993.

Love, Carrie. *Animals: A Visual Encyclopedia*. London: Dorling Kindersley, 2008.

Lynch, Wayne. *Penguins of the World*. 2nd ed. Richmond Hill, ON: Firefly Books, 2007.

Whyman, Kathryn. *The Animal Kingdom: A Guide to Vertebrate Classification and Biodiversity*. Austin, TX: Raintree Steck-Vaughn, 2000.

Websites

http://animals.sandiegozoo.org/
http://coolcosmos.ipac.caltech.edu/image_galleries/ir_zoo/coldwarm.html
http://nationalzoo.si.edu/Animals/
www.tpwd.state.tx.us/kids/wild_things/fish/howdofishbreathe.phtml

With love for my sisters, Molly and Jolie, animal lovers both!—M. L.

To my mom, the library lady—M. G.

Special thank to my editor, Grace Maccarone, for her time and attention to every word.—M. L.

The publisher would like to thank Louis N. Sorkin, B.C.E., American Museum of Natural History, for his expert review of this book.

Text copyright © 2014 by Michelle Lord
Illustrations copyright © 2014 by Michael Garland
All Rights Reserved
HOLIDAY HOUSE is registered in the U.S. Patent and Trademark Office.
Printed and Bound in April 2014 at Toppan Leefung, DongGuan City, China.
The artwork was created with digi-woodcut.
www.holidayhouse.com
First Edition
1 3 5 7 9 10 8 6 4 2

Library of Congress Cataloging-in-Publication Data
Lord, Michelle.
Animal school : what class are you? / by Michelle Lord ; illustrated by Michael Garland. — First edition.
pages cm
Includes bibliographical references.
ISBN 978-0-8234-3045-1 (hardcover)
1. Vertebrates—Juvenile literature. 2. Vertebrates—Classification—Juvenile literature.
3. Animals—Classification—Juvenile literature.
I. Garland, Michael, illustrator. II. Title.
QL605.3L67 2014
596—dc23
2013019680